PYTHON IN A DAY

Richard Wagstaff

Contents

Preface

I have made this book to get you up and running in Python in the fastest time possible. It is simple and short to give you a good, concise base from which you can begin to explore Python.

I have deliberately made sure that each chapter uses separate code so that if you get hopelessly stuck in a chapter, you can move onto the next chapter regardless. However, fixing errors is all part of the learning experience, but don't lose hope and stop learning Python if you cannot fix the errors. Just move onto the next chapter and come back to the problem later.

Note: Google is a great resource for assisting you in pinning down what you may be doing wrong!

1

About Python

"Live as if you were to die tomorrow. Learn as if you were to live forever."

- Mahatma Gandhi

What Is Python?

I will very quickly give you an overview of what Python is. If you have literally no idea what Python is, well then it's a computer programming language.

Here are some reasons why you'll love using Python:

1.   Python is fun
2.   Python is fast
3.   Python is simple
4.   Python is powerful

Using The Book

The purpose of this section is to let you know how

to read and use the book to your best advantage. If the following doesn't make any sense to you, do not worry for now - you can easily refer back to it later.

1.   All code to be put in a script has been formatted in this way:

```
Sample code
```

2.   You will find small text in italics beneath the code boxes that refer to where you can find the script online or in the downloaded files.

3.   Any code that needs to be typed into the console will be like this:

```
>>> some_command
```

4.   Any commands, expressions or parts from the code that are referenced in the book will be highlighted just as this x and this variableName are.

5.   If you ever get stuck with what a word means, check out the jargon buster which is located at the end of the book. I have tried to include as many descriptions for programming words as possible, but if I haven't added something you don't know, then just Google it!

Every example I take you through is available to download from the companion website. You can view them quickly online if you do not want to download them. The code in this book isn't formatted perfectly in all places and is sometimes difficult to read. It is recommended that you use the files online alongside the book, and can be found at the following address:

http://www.inadaybooks.com/files/python/

2

Installation

"Always bear in mind that your own resolution to succeed is more important than any other."

- Abraham Lincoln (16th President of the United States)

Quick Notes

Here I will guide you through installing Python on any Windows, Mac or Linux computer.

First, we need to head to the following website:

http://www.python.org/getit/

We are going to be using Python 2.7.3. Don't let the numbers scare you, it's just the version number.

For Mac

Look for the following link and click on it to

download the file.

*Python 2.7.3 Mac OS X 64-bit/32-bit x86-64/
i386 Installer (for Mac OS X 10.6 and later [2])*

Steps:

1. When it has finished downloading, you need to open the file.
2. You should now see four files. Find the 'Python.mpkg' file and open it up to get to the installation screen.
3. Click through the installation to install Python onto your computer.
4. Now either search for 'IDLE' from the search bar or go to your applications to open it up.

That's us done with install, so now you can skip through to the end of the chapter.

For Windows

Look for the following link and click on it to download the file.

*Python 2.7.3 Windows Installer
(Windows binary -- does not include source)*

Steps:

1. Once the file has been downloaded, double click the file to install onto your computer.
2. Go through the installation steps to install onto your computer.

3. Upon completion, open up a program called IDLE which you have just installed.

That's us done with install, so now you can skip through to the end of the chapter.

For Linux

To install Python, we first need to open up the Terminal. Do this by using the keyboard shortcut 'Ctrl + Alt + T' or look in your applications for Terminal. If for any reason you can't find the Terminal, just search for how to do it on Google.

When the Terminal is open, type the following:

```
$ sudo apt-get install idle
```

Note: Don't type the '$', it's there to show you it's a command to type in the Terminal.

This will install the Python interface and give you a simple code editor to use. You now need to go to your applications and open up a program called 'IDLE'. Alternatively, you can search for IDLE in the search bar to find it quickly.

For more advanced users, note that you can run the Python shell in the terminal by typing in 'python'. To exit the shell, press Ctrl-C. To run Python files, you need to navigate to their location in the terminal, and then then type the following to run it:

```
$ python filename.py
```

3

Python Basics 1

"Learning to write programs stretches your mind, and helps you think better, creates a way of thinking about things that I think is helpful in all domains."

\- Bill Gates (Chairman, Microsoft)

Diving in: Python Basics

Quick note: Always save Python files with the '.py' extension:

filename.py

If IDLE isn't open already, open it up by searching through your programs or applications. You should see the screen shown in Figure 1, which we will now refer to as the 'console'.

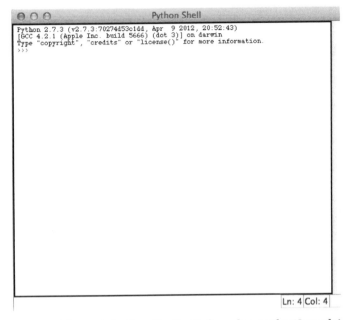

Figure 1: Python Shell – Referred to as the 'Console'

In the console, we can type commands such as:

```
>>> print 'This stuff rocks'
This stuff rocks
```

Note that the >>> that I am putting a statement into the console. The line below the >>> is what the console prints out. So, do not type >>> into the console just the statement after, e.g. print 'This stuff rocks'. If you don't understand what I just said, don't worry! You will get it shortly.

Figure 2 is a screenshot that shows you what I just explained:

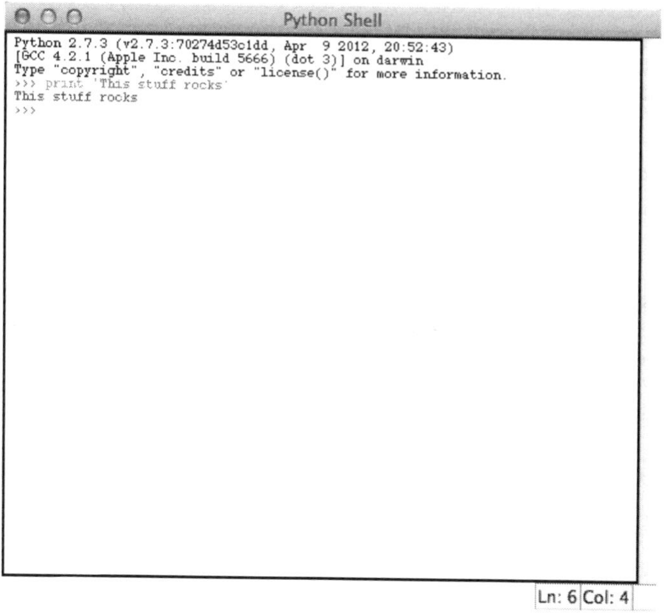

```
Python 2.7.3 (v2.7.3:70274d53c1dd, Apr  9 2012, 20:52:43)
[GCC 4.2.1 (Apple Inc. build 5666) (dot 3)] on darwin
Type "copyright", "credits" or "license()" for more information.
>>> print 'This stuff rocks'
This stuff rocks
>>>
```

Ln: 6 | Col: 4

Figure 2: Using the console

This is what we call returning a value and showing it in the console.

Now try this:

```
>>> print This stuff rocks
```

And we get an error. This is because the text does not have quotation marks around it. Whenever we refer to text, we need to let Python know that it is a *string* by including the text between two quotation marks. Python accepts quotation marks as either (' ') or (" ").

Learning to understand errors is mega important and is all about experience, so when you next see the error 'SyntaxError: invalid syntax', one of your checks can be to make sure you've defined your strings properly.

Introducing Variables

In the console, type the following commands:

```
>>> x = 10
>>> print x
10
```

You will see that the console returns the value '10'. Congratulations, you have just created your first variable!

I know you want more though - you just can't help yourself now!

Now try typing the following commands:

```
>>> y = 2
>>> print(x+y)
12
```

And there you have it, your first piece of maths in Python. Easy, huh? Now try changing it up a bit using the following instead of adding the values:

```
>>> print(x-y)
8
>>> print(x*y)
20
>>> print(x/y)
5
```

You will see that (-) subtracts, (*) multiplies and (/) divides. Great stuff!

One very important thing to note about Python is that it is case-sensitive. For example, type the following into the console:

```
>>> print X
```

This gives the error 'NameError: name 'X' is not defined'. Always make sure you don't mix up your cases!

Data Types

Now would be a good time to introduce the most common data types in Python.

Integer (*int*)

An integer is a whole number, i.e. 1, 4, 6394

Float

A float is a number with a decimal point, I.e. 3.21, 0.3249

Boolean

A boolean is a value that can either be True or False.

String

A sequence of characters that have quotation marks at the beginning and end.

All we need to do is the following when making a variable:

```
>>> some_int_variable = 2
>>> some_float_variable = 1.24
>>> some_boolean_variable = True
>>> some_string_value = "awesome text
here"
```

4

Python Basics 2

"Most good programmers do programming not because they expect to get paid or get adulation by the public, but because it is fun to program."

- Linus Torvalds (The guy behind Linux)

Writing Scripts

In IDLE, go to **File** - **New Window**.

This brings up a text editor that allows you to create Python scripts like the one shown in Figure 3.

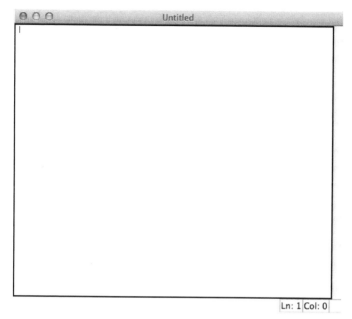

Figure 3: Script editor

Using the code from the previous section, we can put it into a script as shown:

```
x = 10
y = 2

print(x+y)
```

basics2/script_001.py

Before we run the script, we need to save it. To do this, go to File — Save as.

Make sure that you add `.py` to the end of the filename you give it, e.g. `simple_script.py`

Now, to run this script either press F5 or go to 'Run' – 'Run Module'. If you go back to the console, you should see that `12` has been returned by running the script.

Start Commenting

Comments are essential to guiding yourself and others through the program and how different parts work, so it is something I strongly encourage you to do.

Comments are easy to add, just use # for single line comments or ''' for multiple line comments. See below for an example using the previous script:

```
x = 10
y = 2

# Print x + y
print(x+y)
```

basics2/script_002.py

Now, run the file again by pressing 'F5' and make sure it makes no difference to the output. So everything after the # in that line is not read by the script and is mega handy for making notes.

Should you want to use multi line comments just put the text between two ''' and ''' as shown:

```
x = 10
y = 2

''' Prints x + y
to the shell '''
print(x+y)
```

basics2/script_003.py

This allows you to give more descriptive text without the hassle of using the # every time. Remember to close the text with ' ' ' when you finish the comment.

Python Notation

Python has a unique way of structuring code. With Python, you **must** indent when a statement has been made. If you look at the code below, you will see that after the if statement, there is a colon :, and everything within that if statement has been indented. Don't worry about the if statement for now, just make sure you understand that you must indent after a statement has been made.

Note: This will be strange if you have ever programmed in other languages, but stick with it and you'll come to love it.

```
x = 10
y = 2

if x == 10:
    print 'x = 10'
```

basics2/script_004.py

When you want to come out of the statement, you remove the indent and start typing in line with the if statement as shown:

```
if x == 10:
                # In the statement
                print 'x = 10'
                # Still in the statement
```

```
# Not in the statement. Statement finished
```

basics2/script_005.py

With all that, you should be ready to move onto the next section.

Puppet Master: Playing The Strings

"Great coders are today's rockstars"

- will.i.am (Musician, Producer and Entrepreneur)

String Manipulation

First of all, open up a new module window to create our script by going to File – New Window.

You can do fun things with strings. For example, let's make a variable called `name`, and play around a bit with it.

```
>>> name = "Guido"
```

strings/script_001.py

If we wanted to get a specific character from the name, such as the first letter, we do the following:

```
>>> print name[0]
```

strings/script_001.py

The number in the brackets is the index of the character in the string. Try playing around with some different numbers. Remember that the first letter has an index of 0.

We can also do the following:

```
>>> print name.upper()
GUIDO
>>> print name.lower()
guido
>>> print name.capitalize()
Guido
```

strings/script_002.py

Type those into the console and see what happens to the string.

Note that .upper() changes all of the characters in the string to uppercase, and .lower() changes them all to lowercase. Although it appears .capitalize() did nothing, it takes the string and capitalizes the first letter only. As the string was already formatted that way, it made no difference.

Format a Date

Let's say we have a date in string form such as 11/12/2013 and want get the day, month and year from it. Probably the easiest way to do it would be to use the .split() command. Here's how it works:

```
date = "11/12/2013"

# Go through string and split
# where there is a '/'
date_manip = date.split('/')
```

```
# Show the outcome
print date_manip
```

strings/script_003.py

The `.split('/')` command splits the string where the / character appears and then returns each part in date form. More about lists later, but for the purposes of this chapter, we can get the month, day and year from the list by doing the following:

Change:

```
print date_manip
```

strings/script_003.py

To:

```
print date_manip[0]
print date_manip[1]
print date_manip[2]
```

strings/script_004.py

It would be nice if we could know which value is which. To do this we need to write a string and concatenate it to `date_manip[0]` so that it displays the following in the console.

```
Month: 11
```

Now we are going to concatenate a string with the items in the list. Concatenate basically means joining objects together. To do this, you use the + symbol.

So, let's use it to show the month, day and year.

```
print 'Month: ' + date_manip[0]
print 'Day: ' + date_manip[1]
print 'Year: ' + date_manip[2]
```

strings/script_005.py

And try running it. You will see that each of the numbers have the correct text to the left of them.

Note: Make sure you put a space after the colon : in strings like this to give a space to the value your adding to the end of the string.

If you wanted to display this all in a single line in the console, you could do the following:

```
print('Month: ' + date_manip[0] +
      'Day: ' + date_manip[1]
      + 'Year: ' + date_manip[2])
```

strings/script_006.py

Note: I pressed 'Enter' to write on a new line after date_manip[1]. *This helps to keep the code clean and easy to read in this book, but it's not essential for you to do it. Also note that you need brackets surrounding around what you're printing if you use multiple lines.*

Try running the script and observe the outputs in the console. Did you notice what happened? The Day: string is attached to 11 and the Year: string is attached to 12. To fix this, add a full stop and space in the strings as shown:

```
print('Month: ' + date_manip[0] +
      '. Day: ' + date_manip[1]
      + '. Year: ' + date_manip[2])
```

strings/script_007.py

Run the script. Ah, that looks much better now doesn't it?

Note: When doing this be careful that everything is

in string form when concatenate. You can convert to string by using `str(value)`, *and need to be extra careful to convert when concatenating integers.*

Breakdown of String Methods

`.upper()`

Changes string to uppercase

`.lower()`

Changes string to lowercase

`.capitalize()`

Capitalizes the first letter of the string

`.title()`

Capitalizes the first letter of every word in the string

`.swapcase()`

Switches the case of every character in the string

`.strip()`

Removes whitespace, tabs and indents from the string.

6

Make a Statement

"And then it occurred to me that a computer is a stupid machine with the ability to do incredibly smart things, while computer programmers are smart people with the ability to do incredibly stupid things. They are, in short, a perfect match."

- Bill Bryson (best-selling American author)

Statements

The most common statements you will use in Python are:

1. `if`, `else`, `elif`
2. `for` loop
3. `while` loop

For the statements, we need to understand what each of the symbols mean in the following list:

`==`   Is equal to

!=	Not equal to
>	Greater than
<	Less than
>=	Greater than or equal to
<=	Less than or equal to

Now, try running the following in the console:

```
>>> x = 5
>>> print x == 5
True
>>> print x == 4
False
>>> print x < 7
True
```

True means that the statement is correct, and False means that the statement is incorrect. Note that when we're looking at whether a value is equal to another, we use two == rather than the single = sign. Now try the following commands and see what happens:

```
>>> print x > 7
>>> print x != 3
>>> print x >= 5
>>> print x <= 5
>>> print x > 5
```

Once you understand why the console returns True or False, you're well on your way to smashing this chapter. Remember to refer back to the list of statements at the beginning of the chapter if you don't know what the symbols represent.

If, Else and Elif

You have already briefly seen the `if` statement in the previous chapter, and here's how it works:

```
if (some condition):
            <Start code if (some condition) is
True>
            ...
            <End of code>
```

Example

If the condition is `True` (correct), then Python will run the code in the indented space. If the condition is `False` (incorrect) then it will skip the code in the indented space.

We can expand on the statement and include an `else` statement as shown:

```
If (some condition):
            < Indented space runs if (some
condition) is True >
Else:
            < Indented space runs if (some
condition) is False >
```

Example

Now, instead of ignoring the `if` statement as it did previously if the condition was `False`, it now runs the code that is indented in the else part.

The last thing to add is the `elif` statement, which stands for 'else if'. You can see how this works below:

```
if (some condition 1):
              < This indented space runs if
(some condition 1) is True
elif (some condition 2):
              < This indented space runs if
(some condition 2) is True and some condition
1) is False >
else:
              < This indented space runs if
(some condition) is False >
```

Example

From this, you can see that the `elif` statement will only run if the statements before it are False. You can use as many `elif` statements as you like!

So, how does this work in Python code?

Well, firstly open up a new window for our statement script by pressing Ctrl-N or File – New Window.

Let's take our original example and add the following statements. Remember that # is a comment and everything in that line after the # will be ignored by Python.

```
# Define the variables
x = 10

# Start if statement
if x == 10:
              print 'x = 10'

# If x does not equal 10, but equals 9 run this
elif x == 9:
              print 'x = 9'
```

```
# If it's not equal to 10 or 9, run this
else:
                print 'x does not equal 9 or 10'
```
statements/script_001.py

Run the script and you should see it return x = 10. Now try changing the x variable to 9 and running the script again:

```
x = 9
```
statements/script_002.py

This should return x = 9 in the console.

Now, see for yourself what happens when you change x to 1:

```
x = 1
```
statements/script_003.py

7

Going Loopy

"Learning to code is useful no matter what your career ambitions are."

- Arianna Huffington (Founder of the Huffington Post)

The 'while' Loop

There are two types of loops in Python, the `for` loop and the `while` loop. I almost always use only the `for` loop, but I do use the while loop on occasion.

Before you start, open up a new window for the scripts in this chapter.

A basic while loop looks like this:

```
# Start counter at 0
counter = 0

# While 'counter' is less than or equal to 5,
# run the loop
```

```
while counter < 5:
            # Show counter value
            print counter
            # Shortcut to increase counter by
1
            counter = counter + 1
```

loops/script_001.py

So, what the loop is doing is iterating the code inside the loop until the counter variable is greater than 5. The counter gets increased by 1 on every iteration by the `counter = counter + 1` expression. So, it's basically running the following script without us having to type it all out:

```
print counter
counter = counter + 1
print counter
counter = counter + 1
print counter
counter = counter + 1
print counter
counter = counter + 1
print counter
counter = counter + 1
```

Example: What the loop automates

And as you can see, that's a fair few lines of code. For anything repetitive in computer programming, make the computer do it for you. Your time is much too valuable!

Python has a nifty little shortcut that allows you to increment quickly by a certain value. To do this, simply change:

```
counter = counter + 1
```

loops/script_001.py

To:

```
counter += 1
```

loops/script_002.py

Note: You can change the 1 to any value you want.

If we remove the command that adds 1 to the counter variable and ran the code, Python would get stuck in an infinite loop. This is something you need to be extremely careful about when using while loops, and it's the main reason I try to avoid them where possible.

If you ever do get stuck in an infinite loop, press Ctrl-C to stop the script.

The 'for' Loop

An alternative to while loop is the for loop. To create exactly the same loop as above, we can write the following:

```
# Run loop in range 0 - 5
# Counter changes automatically in each
iteration
for counter in range(0,5):
              # Show the value of counter
              print counter
```

loops/script_003.py

This does exactly the same thing as the while loop, but you don't need to start with counter = 0 or worry about increasing the counter every iteration.

Therefore, you cannot get stuck in an infinite loop when using a `for` loop. In this case, `range(0,5)` is an inbuilt Python function that will return values from 0 to 5, and makes the `counter` variable equal to each number in each iteration.

Note that `range(0,5)` returns the values 0, 1, 2, 3 and 4, so only values up to, but not including 5.

8

Lists

"Coders change the world. They build new, amazing things faster than ever before. Anyone with imagination can learn to write code."

- Jeff Wilke (SVP Consumer Business, Amazon.com)

Starting Lists

Lists can be used in Python to store information such as strings, numbers and just about any other data!

Let's get straight to it. Making a list is simple; all you need to do is make an expression such as.

```
name_of_list = [list_item_1, list_item_2]
```

The most important parts are the brackets that have the list items sandwiched in between them and the comma to separate each list item.

We are going to create a list of some pretty

amazing programmers using our new found knowledge.

In a new window, type the following:

```
# Create the list of epic programmers
epic_programmer_list = ["Tim Berners-Lee",
                        "Guido van Rossum",
                        "Linus Torvalds",
                        "Larry Page",
                        "Sergey Brin",]
```

lists/script_001.py

Note that after each comma I pressed 'Enter' to write on a new line. This helps to keep the code clean and easy to read in this book, but it's not essential for you to do it.

We want to display them all with some added text in the console, so let's try adding the following snippet of code and running the script:

Note: To recap, the + symbol concatenates (joins) the item to the end of the text

```
# print to console
print "Epic programmers: " +
epic_programmer_list
```

loops/script_002.py

Ah, we have an error that says TypeError: cannot concatenate 'str' and 'list' objects.

This error means that it cannot add a string to the list object. To fix this we must take the items out of the list before we concatenate them with another string. Try this instead:

```
# print to console
print "An epic programmer: " +
epic_programmer_list[0]
```

loops/script_003.py

Ah, that works! It now prints `An epic programmer: Tim Berners-Lee` to the console. The brackets at the end refer to the index in the list, so `[0]` on the end of the `epic_programmer_list` refers to the first value in the list. If we changed `[0]` to `[1]`, it would grab the second item in the list, which in this case would be `Guido van Rossum`. Feel free to play around with it by changing the numbers. Blame computer scientists for starting counting from `0` and not `1`! Stick with it and you'll get to like it.

What if we want all of the programmers to print out? Well, try this:

```
# Print to console
print "An epic programmer: " +
epic_programmer_list[0]
print "An epic programmer: " +
epic_programmer_list[1]
print "An epic programmer: " +
epic_programmer_list[2]
print "An epic programmer: " +
epic_programmer_list[3]
print "An epic programmer: " +
epic_programmer_list[4]
```

loops/script_004.py

Run the program and check the console. You should see that all of the programmers appear that we put into the list in the beginning.

Changing Lists

Now, what if you felt that one of the programmers was unworthy of the list and you wanted to change one of them? Unlikely, but I'll show you how to do it anyway:

```
# Create the list of epic programmers
epic_programmer_list = ["Tim Berners-Lee",
                        "Guido van Rossum",
                        "Linus Torvalds",
                        "Larry Page",
                        "Sergey Brin",]
epic_programmer_list[4] = "Me"
print epic_programmer_list
```

loops/script_004.py

So this grabs the item at index 4, which was Sergey Brin, and changes it to Me. If you run the script, you will see that you have replaced Sergey Brin with yourself in your list of epic programmers. Frankly, I think that's a little harsh so let's fix that by adding yourself to the list and keeping **all** of the other epic programmers!

Firstly, remove the last snippet where you replaced yourself for Sergey Brin, harsh... anyway, he forgives you for now as you are fixing it by using the .append expression. To add an item to the list, insert the following code into your script:

```
# Add myself to the end of the list
epic_programmer_list.append("Me")
```

loops/script_005.py

And now you need to add another print to show yourself in the console.

```
# Add this line to show myself in the console
print "An epic programmer: " +
epic_programmer_list[5]
```

loops/script_005.py

Try running that and you should see yourself in the list of epic programmers in the console. That's pretty awesome!

Going Loopy with Lists

But we can make this even more awesome. Did you find it a little boring and repetitive typing out the print for every line? I sure did. Well, let's remove the repetitive stuff and make the computer work for us as computers are generally brilliant at doing incredibly boring stuff really quickly.

The for loop is perfect for this situation. Get rid of all those print lines you did and add the following for loop to the script:

```
# Looping through each item in
epic_programmer_list
for programmer in epic_programmer_list:
    # Print the programmers' name to console
    print programmer
```

loops/script_006.py

Run that and marvel at its simplicity! Damn that was easy.

Here's what happens; the for statement loops around each item in the epic_programmer_list, and makes the programmer variable equal to the item. Inside the for loop I included the command `print` `programmer` which prints out the `programmer` variable that is passed into the loop each time.

Imagine if you had a list of 100 programmers, it would get pretty tedious creating separate lines to print out each of them! Now, we need to make just one more modification to the print to make it like it was before adding the `for` loop.

Change:

```
print programmer
```

loops/script_006.py

To:

```
print "An epic programmer: " + programmer
```

loops/script_007.py

Run it. Purrrfect!

Lists with Numbers

Lists do not just work for strings, they work well for all sorts of objects too. The following example uses numbers. First, we create a list with numbers in it and then create another `for` loop that loops through each number in the list and does something to it. In this case, we will put each number to the power of 2. The `for` loop works in exactly the same way as the last example, with the only difference being that it passes a number into the loop instead of a string:

```
# Create list of numbers
number_list = [1,2,3,4,5]

# Loop each number in number_list
for x in number_list:
    # Print each number to the power of 2
    print x**2
```

loops/script_008.py

Run the script and look what happens in the console.

What if we wanted to go one further and store these values in a new list? Well that's pretty simple too. Create a new empty list by using empty square brackets e.g. `empty_list = []`. Now, when the `for` loop does each iteration we can make it append the number to the power of 2 to the empty list. This is exactly the same as the method we used for adding you to the end of the `epic_programmer_list`.

First, we need to add an empty list. We will name it `empty_number_list` and place it beneath the `number_list`:

```
empty_number_list = []
```

loops/script_009.py

Next, we add the expression `.append` into the `for` loop. Remove the `print` command and replace it with:

```
# Append each number to the power of 2
# to the empty_number_list
empty_number_list.append(x**2)
```

loops/script_009.py

And finally add this line after the `for` loop to print the final list:

```
print empty_number_list
```

loops/script_009.py

So, the entire script looks like the following:

```
# Create list of numbers
number_list = [1,2,3,4,5]
empty_number_list = []

# Loop each number in number_list
for x in number_list:
    # Append each number to the power of 2
    # to the empty_number_list
    empty_number_list.append(x**2)

print empty_number_list
```

loops/script_009.py

To summarise, the loop takes the empty list `empty_number_list` and adds the `x**2` value to the end of the list. We then print out the entire list with the expression `print empty_number_list`.

Pretty tidy, huh?

With all that, you should be ready to move onto the next section.

9

Writing a Dictionary

"Everybody in this country should learn how to program a computer because it teaches you how to think."

- Steve Jobs (co-founder, chairman, and CEO of Apple Inc)

How Dictionaries Work

Writing a whole dictionary doesn't take as long as you might think! Again, make a new file for this chapter.

Dictionaries are a more advanced type of list. To create a dictionary, use curly braces {} and do the following:

```
>>> dictionary_name = {'item_1':1,
'item_2':2, 'item_3':3 }
```

dictionary/script_001.py

To get information out of the dictionary, we can

refer to it as follows:

```
>>> print dictionary_name['item_1']
```
dictionary/script_001.py

This searches the dictionary for `item_1` and returns the data that it's linked to, in this case it returns `1`.

Writing Dictionaries

The following example shows a way in which dictionaries can be used:

Let's take our list of epic programmers from the previous section and link their names to their email addresses. Disclaimer: I don't believe these are their real email addresses, but who knows!

First, create a dictionary called `epic_programmer_dict`:

```
epic_programmer_dict = {'Tim Berners-Lee' :
'tbl@gmail.com',
                        'Guido van Rossum' :
'gvr@gmail.com',
                        'Linus Torvalds':
'lt@gmail.com',
                        }
```
dictionary/script_002.py

Run the script and then in the console make a quick check to make sure it's working:

```
>>> print epic_programmer_dict
```
dictionary/script_002.py

Now we're going to go a bit deeper and return an

email address for the programmer `Tim Berners-Lee` by typing the following into the console:

```
>>> print epic_programmer_dict['Tim
Berners-Lee']
```

dictionary/script_002.py

Yep, that returns his email address! If you get an error, make sure that the strings match correctly and that all of the code is exactly the same as above.

Now, we can change their email address by the adding the following statement:

```
# Adds a different email address
epic_programmer_dict['Tim Berners-Lee'] =
'tim@gmail.com'
print 'New email for Tim: ' +
epic_programmer_dict['Tim Berners-Lee']
```

dictionary/script_003.py

For the eagle eyed among you, you may have noticed that we have fewer epic programmers in that dictionary than in our previous list. Well, instead of changing the dictionary statement at the beginning, we can add a new programmer and email address by typing the following snippet into our script:

```
# Add Larry Page and his email to the
dictionary
epic_programmer_dict['Larry Page'] =
'lp@gmail.com'
```

dictionary/script_004.py

By observing this expression, we can see that we are referencing the `epic_programmer_dict` and then adding square braces `[]` with a string in between. The string inside the brackets gets added to the dictionary and this is you need to search for when searching the dictionary.

This expression is simple and provides us with a very useful way to add information to the dictionary at any point in the script. We should check that Larry Page was added correctly, so run the script and try searching for his name and see what happens:

```
>>> print epic_programmer_dict
```

dictionary/script_004.py

After running that, we can see that Larry Page was added to the list. Now go ahead and add yourself and Sergey Brin to the dictionary using the same method. Use 'sb@gmail.com' for Sergey's email address.

What if we want to delete something in the dictionary? That's pretty simple. Just use the following code:

```
# Delete Sergey Brin from the dictionary
del epic_programmer_dict['Sergey Brin']
```

dictionary/script_005.py

If you didn't add Sergey Brin to the dictionary, then you will receive the error `KeyError: 'Sergey Brin'`. This means that the item 'Sergey Brin' does not exist in the dictionary, and therefore cannot be deleted. It has come to my attention that we seem to keep removing Sergey Brin from our epic programmer lists, so I think you should try out deleting someone else for once! To do this, simply type a different name in between the brackets in the `del` command. Don't forget your quotation marks as their name is a string!

Well, that's covered Python dictionaries so you should be ready to move on to the next section.

10

Learn to Function

The computing scientist's main challenge is not to get confused by the complexities of his own making.

- E. W. Dijkstra (Computer Scientist)

How Functions Work

Functions are great. They save space and make things tidy meaning they are just plain brilliant. In Python, functions are pretty simple when you know how to do them.

What is a function?

A function is something where you put values in and get something out in return. The function can be used whenever you like in the script by 'calling' it.

Programming functions

The code for a function in Python looks like this:

```
def someFunction(< input variables >):
          < Do stuff here with input
variables >
          return < some value >
```

Example: Outline of a function

When we create a function, we need to put `def` as shown in the example. This lets Python know that we are making a function.

In this example, `someFunction` is the name of your function. You can choose any name you like, but make sure that you use no spaces or special characters. Numbers are allowed, but cannot be the first character of the name.

The `< input variables >` in the brackets are variables that are 'passed' into the function. This will make more sense in a minute. You can pass as many variables as you like into a function.

The return line is where you put what you want outputted from the function, i.e. `< some value >`.

Fun with Functions

Before we start, open up a new window to input the code for this chapter.

Let's try an example where we put two variables, `x` and `y`, into a function called `letsAdd`. Inside the function, we will make `x` and `y` add together, and then output the value:

```
def letsAdd(x,y):
            addition = x + y
            return addition
```

functions/script_001.py

As you can see, we made a variable called addition inside the function to add the x and y values together. This variable is then returned as the output of the function.

Now, let's check our function is working properly and add the following line to the script:

```
print letsAdd(3, 5)
```

functions/script_001.py

This makes x = 3 and y = 5 as the input variables. Alternatively, we could run the print line in the console.

Anything that is created inside the function does not get put into your script unless it's in the return expression. Try it out by modifying your script to the following:

```
def letsAdd(x,y):
            addition = x + y
            someValue = 10
            return addition

print letsAdd(3, 5)
print someValue
```

functions/script_002.py

When you run this, you get an error stating that NameError: name 'someValue' is not defined. This shows you that any variable made inside the function does not exist outside of the function.

Now, let's try putting `someValue = 5` at the very top of the script before the function:

```
someValue = 5
```
functions/script_003.py

Run the script again and you will see that the console prints 5. This shows that `someValue` went untouched when the function was called.

Now, let's try making some more functions. Try writing the following code to make a subtraction function and print the result:

```
# Make function called subtraction
def subtraction(x,y):
            # Make subtract variable equal to
x - y

            subtract = x - y

            # Return subtract variable
            return subtract

print subtraction(10, 4)
```
functions/script_004.py

Run this and we should get 6 outputted to the console.

We can ramp this up a bit - check out the following function:

```
def moreSubtraction(x,y, z):
            # Make subtract variable equal to
x - y - z

            subtract = x - y - z

            # Return subtract variable
            return subtract
```

functions/script_004.py

This time we need to pass three variables into the function, otherwise Python will return an error message. To make it run correctly, type the following:

```
print moreSubtraction(40, 3, 11)
```

functions/script_004.py

In this case, $x = 40$, $y = 3$, $z = 11$ in the function.

Hopefully functions are starting to click now. Go ahead and make your own; I recommend making the following functions:

1. A multiplication formula
2. A division formula

My functions for multiplication and division can be found by viewing *functions/script_005.py* on our website at:

http://www.inadaybooks.com/files/python/

Handy hint for division: If your division is being rounded to the nearest whole number it means you have it in integer mode. To fix this simply use the following line:

```
divide = float(x)/float(y)
```

Hint for showing decimal place when dividing

This will give make give the divide variable with decimal places.

Remember that if you ever get stuck you can refer to the project scripts on the website. You can sign up here:

www.inadaybooks.com/files/

Built-in Functions

The following is some cool stuff Python can do and has built in.

The `len()` function gets the length of whatever you pass into it. In the example below, Python will count the number of characters in the string and return it for you. Play around with your own strings and see what happens!

```
>>> length = len("How epic are built-in
functions, huh?")
>>> print length
37
```

functions/script_006.py

The `str()` function turns whatever is passed to it into a string. For example, you can convert any integer, float or boolean into a string by calling the string command as follows:

```
>>> x = 23
>>> print str(x)
23
>>> x = 2.32
>>> print str(x)
```

2.32

functions/script_007.py

The `float()` function requires whatever passed into it to be converted into a fractional number, which allows for decimal points to be shown:

```
>>> y = float(40)/float(7)
>>> print y
5.71428571429
```

functions/script_007.py

And if you want to convert the float into an integer, then simply do the following:

```
>>> yInt = int(y)
>>> print yInt
5
```

functions/script_007.py

You may have noticed that before it returned the value `5.714`... and `yInt` returns `5`. Therefore, the `int()` function strips the decimal points away, and does not round to the nearest whole number. If we want to round, we can do:

```
>>> print round(y)
6.0
```

functions/script_007.py

This gives us `6.0`. This still isn't an integer though. We can fix that by doing the rounding first, then converting to an integer as shown:

```
>>> print int(round(y))
6
```

functions/script_007.py

That   does   the   trick!

11
Importing Modules

"Any fool can write code that a computer can understand. Good programmers write code that humans can understand"

- Martin Fowler (Programming Expert and Consultant)

How Modules Work

Python allows you to make modules that contain objects such as functions that you can 'borrow' and use in a new script.

To start with, we will use a built-in module called `math`. To use it in our script, we need to add the following snippet of code to the top of the script:

```
import math
```

modules/script_001.py

This command will import all of the functions that

are included in the math module into our script. As Python doesn't have any inbuilt square root function, we must import the math module to perform it. To get the square root of 16, we use the following expression:

```
print math.sqrt(16)
```

modules/script_001.py

And if we run the script, we will see that it returns `4.0` to the console.

But let's not stop there - if the square root function is all we need from the math module, then we're wasting computing power by importing all of the functions. So, let's change this a little:

```
from math import sqrt

print sqrt(16)
```

modules/script_002.py

This time, notice that I made a slight change to the import expression. This change means that the `sqrt()` function does not require the `math.` section before it. Should we want to import more functions from math, we simply add them to the import statement as shown, with a comma separating the importing functions:

```
from math import sqrt, exp

print sqrt(16)
print exp(2)
```

modules/script_003.py

`exp()` calculates 'e' to the power of something. 'e'

is a constant that is approximately equal 2.71828, but where it comes from is beyond the scope of this book, and probably not something you need to know.

You can find more math functions at the following link:

http://docs.python.org/2/library/math.html

Make Your Own

Making your own modules full of functions is a great way to tidy up your Python scripts and stop repeating yourself with similar functions. Fortunately for us, custom Modules aren't too difficult to create and import into our own scripts.

Start by making a new module and name it `smallMathsModule.py`. Type in the following:

```
# Import the function randint from the random
module
from random import randint

def multiplyBy5(x):
            return 5 * x

def add5(x):
            return x + 5

def randomAdd(x):
            # Get a random integer between 0
and 10
            y = randint(0, 10)
            return x + y
```

modules/smallMathsModule.py

The biggest new thing in this script is using the random module and the function `randint()`. The `randint()` function gets a random integer value in a range of our choosing. In this script, `randint()` gets a random value between 0 and 10.

So now we have three different functions that we will be able to import and use in another module. So, make a new script and save it in the same folder as `smallMathsModule.py`:

```python
# Import our module
import smallMathsModule

# multiplyBy5 function
print smallMathsModule.multiplyBy5(3)

# add5 function
print smallMathsModule.add5(9)

# randomAdd function
print smallMathsModule.randomAdd(8)
```

modules/script_004.py

Now run it.

Run the script as you will see that you have successfully used the functions from `smallMathsModule.py` in our script. Just epic.

12

Make a Program

"Our policy at Facebook is literally to hire as many talented engineers as we can find. There just aren't enough people who are trained and have these skills today"

- Mark Zuckerberg (Founder, Facebook)

Getting Started

Now we're going to create a simple program that takes you through some of the techniques we've learnt in the book. It's entirely up to you how you approach this. Before I show each section of the code I will state what we're doing, so should you like to try it yourself before referring to the code in this book, go ahead.

Now would be a good time to note that code doesn't have to be the same to get the same output. If your method of getting the same result is different from mine, don't worry! Also, don't worry for now how you get to the result as it's great that you're able to reach it in the first place. There may come a time where you have to optimise your code for speed and efficiency, but that is beyond the scope of this book.

The first thing to do is create a new file for the program.

Overview

This program will grab information such as telephone numbers, email addresses, etc by inputting a name into the console.

Firstly, we will create a dictionary so that we can easily handle information such as telephone numbers and email addresses being attached to someone's name. Now, let's start by making a new file, adding the dictionary and checking that the dictionary works properly:

```
# Our epic programmer dict from before
epic_programmer_dict = {
            'Tim Berners-Lee' :
'tbl@gmail.com',
            'Guido van Rossum' :
'gvr@gmail.com',
            'Linus Torvalds': 'lt@gmail.com',
            'Larry Page' : 'lp@gmail.com',
            'Sergey Brin' : 'sb@gmail.com',
            }
print epic_programmer_dict
```

program/script_001.py

Playing with the Dictionary

Run the file and confirm that it runs correctly. Now, we want both their email address and number to be added to the dictionary, so add a list to where there email address is currently. See the following code:

```python
# Our epic programmer dict from before
epic_programmer_dict = {
    'Tim Berners-Lee' : ['tbl@gmail.com', 111],
    'Guido van Rossum' : ['gvr@gmail.com',
222],
    'Linus Torvalds': ['lt@gmail.com', 333],
    'Larry Page' : ['lp@gmail.com', 444],
    'Sergey Brin' : ['sb@gmail.com', 555]
    }
print epic_programmer_dict
```

program/script_002.py

Run the file again to check it works. If you got any errors, make sure you fix them now!

Now, let's see what happens when we request one of the programmers from the dictionary by running the following in the console:

```python
>>> print epic_programmer_dict['Tim
Berners-Lee']
['tbl@gmail.com', 111]
```

program/script_003.py

You should see that it returns the list we defined. If we wanted to go into the list to grab one of the values we can add brackets to the end of the command with the list index like so:

```python
>>> print epic_programmer_dict['Tim
Berners-Lee'][1]
```

```
111
```

program/script_003.py

Try running it and check that the outcome is `111`. This expression works by getting the object in the dictionary for `'Tim Berners-Lee'` which is a list. Then the `[1]` on the end gets the second item in the list that it found. Remember that Python is configured to start indexing from `0`.

An alternative way of achieving the same result is to make the list that gets returned equal to a variable. This allows us to grab items from the by putting their index in square brackets at the end of the variable name shown:

```
programmer = epic_programmer_dict['Tim Berners-
Lee']
print programmer[1]
```

program/script_003.py

I prefer this method as it's easier for me to read and understand, but it's probably just personal preference. If you have a long list, it's probably best to do it the way I prefer so that Python doesn't have to keep looking up `'Tim Berners-Lee'` every time you want to find a piece of his data. For this small dictionary and list it doesn't make much difference to the power required.

Entering a Name

Now we need to figure out how to let the user enter a name and show them the person's information. To do this, I am going to introduce you to the `raw_input()` function. All you need to do is put a prompt between the brackets and make it equal to a variable as shown:

```
personsName = raw_input('Please enter a name:
')
print personsName
```

program/script_004.py

Now, try running that and check the console. You will see the prompt `Please enter a name:`. Go ahead and type in your name and press enter. You will see that the console returns the text you typed in.

As we want to get the person's information from the dictionary and show it to the user, we need to search the dictionary for the variable personsName. To do this, add the following snippet:

```
personsInfo = epic_programmer_dict[personsName]
print personsInfo
```

program/script_005.py

Try running the code again and entering a name. If you entered anything other than a name in the dictionary, you will get a key error. This is something that needs fixing as we can't have the user being shown a red error message saying the program failed.

Manipulating the Error

Instead of the red error message, we want to return a string that tells the user the name cannot be found. To do this, we will use a `try` `except` statement which deals with expressions that show up as errors. It's easier for me to show you how it works in the code:

```
# Looks up the name in the epic dictionary
try:
            # Tries the following lines of
texts, and if
            # there are no errors then it runs
            personsInfo =
epic_programmer_dict[personsName]
            print personsInfo
except:
            # If there are errors, then this
code gets run.
            print 'No information found for
that name'
```

program/script_006.py

Try running it again with a name that is not in the list and you will see that the error message has been replaced with the string 'No information found for that name'. If you type in a name exactly that is in the epic programmer's dictionary, you will see that their information is shown.

More User Friendly

You may have noticed that you have to type in the person's name exactly in the same format as it is in the dictionary. For example, if you searched for 'liNUs torvalds' in the dictionary, it would say that there is no information found.

We need a method of looking through the dictionary for the names no matter what format the user inputs them as. Let's do this by first changing all the uppercase letters in the dictionary to lowercase like so:

```
epic_programmer_dict = {
            'tim berners-lee' :
['tbl@gmail.com', 111],
            'guido van rossum' :
['gvr@gmail.com', 222],
            'linus torvalds': ['lt@gmail.com',
333],
            'larry page' : ['lp@gmail.com',
444],
            'sergey brin' : ['sb@gmail.com',
555]
            }
```

program/script_006.py

Now, if we convert the input to all lowercase characters as well, we can search through the dictionary and grab the right person no matter how the user inputted their name. We can do this by adding `.lower()` to the variable `personsName` as shown:

```
personsName = raw_input('Please enter a name:
').lower()
```

program/script_007.py

Now run the script and try typing in a name in the dictionary with varying upper and lowercase characters such as `'seRGey bRIN'` and you will see that it still finds his information.

Format the Output

We need to make the outputted data look pretty so the user knows what each piece of data is. Let's print out the name of the person they searched for, their email address and their phone number. To do this, we need to modify the `try except` statement to the following:

```
# Looks up the name in the epic dictionary
try:
            # Tries the following lines of
texts, and if
            # there are no errors then it runs
            personsInfo =
epic_programmer_dict[personsName]
            print 'Name: ' + personsName
            print 'Email: ' + personsInfo[0]
            print 'Number: ' + personsInfo[1]
except:
            # If there are errors, then this
code gets run.
            print 'No information found for
that name'
```

program/script_008.py

And run the code. Hmm, something strange seems to be happening. It's returning `No information found for that name` after the email address has been printed. This is because the expression `print 'Number: ' + personsInfo[1]` is producing an error. So, to find out what's causing the error, go into the console and run the line:

```
>>> print 'Number: ' + personsInfo[1]
```

program/script_009.py

This produces the error `cannot concatenate 'str' and 'int' objects`. So, this means that `personsInfo[1]` needs to be changed to a string before it can be added to the string. To fix this, we need to covert the integer to a string by changing:

```
print 'Number: ' + personsInfo[1]
```

program/script_009.py

To:

```
print 'Number: ' + str(personsInfo[1])
```

program/script_009.py

Try running that and confirm that it fixes the issue.

We can make another improvement by displaying the programmers' first and last name with uppercase first letters. To do this, we need to use the `.title()` expression like so:

```
print 'Name: ' + personsName.title()
```

program/script_009.py

Run the script again and check it works correctly.

Make a Loop

Now, if the user wants to search for another programmer, they are going to have to run the script again. Let's simplify this a bit by asking them if they want to search for another programmer before the script stops running. Here we will use a while loop and take a response from the user as to whether they want to continue searching.

Let's start by making a while loop. We will make the variable `userWantsMore` to determine when the user has finished searching for programmers:

```
userWantsMore = True
while userWantsMore = True:
              # Code goes here
              userWantsMore = False
```

program/script_009.py

Try running the script. If you did what I did, you will get an error. This is without doubt the most common error I make in Python. We always need to watch out that when using statements that we use two equals signs == instead of one when we're asking if a value is equal to another. So change the while line to:

```
while userWantsMore == True:
```

program/script_009.py

Now, we need to put the code that gets the information inside the while loop. I decided to make it a function to keep the while loop as clean as possible. I have included the entire script for you below to see what I did. The parts to look at are the function `searchPeople` and how I've moved the `personsName` expression into the while loop:

```
# Our epic programmer dict
epic_programmer_dict = {
    'tim berners-lee' : ['tbl@gmail.com', 111],
    'guido van rossum' : ['gvr@gmail.com',
222],
    'linus torvalds': ['lt@gmail.com', 333],
    'larry page' : ['lp@gmail.com', 444],
    'sergey brin' : ['sb@gmail.com', 555]
```

```
    }


def searchPeople(personsName):
            # Looks up the name in the epic
dictionary
            try:
                    # Tries the following lines
of texts,
                    # and if there aren't any
errors
                    # then it runs
                    personsInfo =
epic_programmer_dict[personsName]
                    print 'Name: ' +
personsName.title()
                    print 'Email: ' +
personsInfo[0]
                    print 'Number: ' +
str(personsInfo[1])
            except:
                    # If there are errors, then
this code gets run.
                    print 'No information found
for that name'

userWantsMore = True
while userWantsMore == True:
            # Asks user to input persons name
            personsName = raw_input('Please
enter a name: ').lower()

            # Run our new function
searchPeople with what was
            # typed in
            searchPeople(personsName)
```

```
            userWantsMore = False
```

program/script_010.py

Hint: When putting lots of indents in, instead of pressing Tab for every line highlight all of what you want indented and then press 'Tab'.

Run the script and make sure you can get the programmers details from the dictionary after input.

The next step is asking the user whether they want to search for another programmer. For this we will ask them to input either y (yes), or n (no), and based on this value we will either step out of the loop or continue. To do this, we will use an 'if' statement and add it to our while loop like so:

```
            # See if user wants to search
again
            searchAgain = raw_input('Search
again? (y/n)')

            # Look at what they reply and act
accordingly
            if searchAgain == 'y':
                # userWantsMore stays as
true so loop repeats
                userWantsMore = True

            elif searchAgain == 'n':
                # userWantsMore turns to
False to stop loop
                userWantsMore = False

            else:
```

```
                # user inputs an invalid
response, so we quit anyway
                print "I dont understand
what you mean, quitting"
                userWantsMore = False
```

program/script_011.py

To break this down for you:

The `searchAgain` variable asks the user if they want to proceed. It offers two responses, `y` or `n`.

The `if` statement looks at what was typed in. If the user enters `y`, then the `userWantsMore` variable stays as `True` and the loop goes round again. If the user enters `n`, the `userWantsMore` variable turns to `False` which causes the loop to stop, and the script to stop running. If they type something else, we will stop the script anyway just in case for whatever reason they get stuck in the loop. To do this, we make the `userWantsMore` variable equal to `False`.

And there's our simple little program! Once you make one feature, just add another feature and build your programs up from there. This is how pretty much everything is programmed and before you know it, you'll be stuck with thousands of lines of code wondering what on earth have I done?!!

Thank You!

Just to say a massive thank you for taking the time to read the book. I really hope you got some really useful stuff out of it and can now do some programming in Python. There are many, many more things for you to learn, but hopefully I have given you a good base from which you can blossom.

So, where do you go from here? Well, I would start off by making a couple of your own little programs. When you get stuck because something doesn't work or you don't know how to do it, search on Google or look in this book for the answer. I can guarantee you that you will discover new things about Python as you start making your own programs.

What to do next? I have thoroughly enjoyed writing the book, and I hope you enjoyed reading it too. If you feel like the book was worthwhile to you, then please leave a review on Amazon so that others can get good use out of the book. It would also help me out too!

You could also try out a different programming language. At the time of printing, I have released the following books:

Ruby In A Day

HTML & CSS In A Day

Thank You!

You can check the website http://inadaybooks.com for new books and updates!

If you ever need to reach me to ask any questions, have feedback or suggestions for the book, then get in touch by emailing me at:

rich@inadaybooks.com

Once again, **thank you** for purchasing this book!

Jargon Buster

Array

Same thing as a list. See Chapter Eight for learning about lists.

Boolean

Has a value of either True or False. You must remember to capitalize the first letter otherwise Python will scream at you.

Concatenate

Basically means joining items together. To do this, you use the + symbol. In my opinion a complex word for a simple task.

Console

The place where you run your Python stuff. See Chapter Three for an image of the console. Also known as the shell.

Expression
In this book it generally means a line of code.

Function
A function is a reusable piece of code where you can put values in and get something out depending on the input.

Float
A floating point. Primary use is to give decimal points.

IDLE
IDLE is an Integrated DeveLopment Environment for Python. It contains an editor and a shell to get Python up and running.

Integer
A whole number, e.g. 1, 4, 82.

Loop
A piece of code that is repeated until a specific condition has been reached.

Shell
I refer to the shell in this book as the console. See

console.

Statement
Examples include is equal to (==), is not equal to (!=) is greater than (>) and so on. Read up about these in Chapter Six.

String
A sequence of characters.

Variable
A variable is something that contains a specific value or object.

Copyright © 2013 by Richard Wagstaff

http://www.inadaybooks.com/